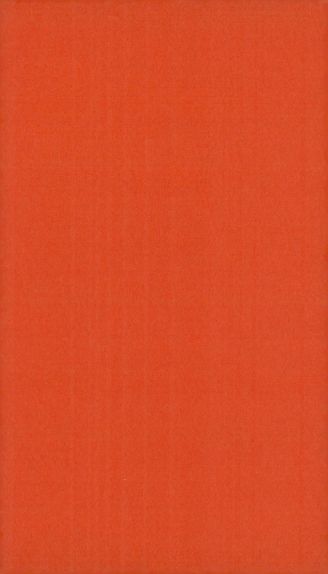

Shakespeare

JOHANN GOTTFRIED HERDER

Shakespeare

*Translated, edited, and with an introduction
by Gregory Moore*

PRINCETON & OXFORD

PRINCETON UNIVERSITY PRESS

Published by Princeton University Press,
41 William Street,
Princeton, New Jersey 08540
In the United Kingdom: Princeton University Press,
3 Market Place, Woodstock,
Oxfordshire OX20 1SY

All Rights Reserved

LIBRARY OF CONGRESS CATALOGING-IN-PUBLICATION DATA
Herder, Johann Gottfried, 1744–1803.
Shakespeare / Johann Gottfried Herder ; translated, edited,
and with an introduction by Gregory Moore.
p. cm.
"First published in 1773, as one of five contributions to a
pamphlet edited by Herder himself and entitled Von deutscher
Art und Kunst (On German Character and Art)" — T.p. verso.
Includes bibliographical references and index.
ISBN: 978-0-691-13535-9 (hardcover : acid-free paper)
1. Shakespeare, William, 1564–1616—Criticism and interpretation.
I. Moore, Gregory, 1972– II. Title.
PR2978.H45   2008
822.3′3—dc22   2007025547

British Library Cataloging-in-Publication Data is available

This book has been composed in Bembo
and Centaur Display

Printed on acid-free paper. ∞

press.princeton.edu

Printed in the United States of America

1 3 5 7 9 10 8 6 4 2

Contents

Introduction   GREGORY MOORE

Shakespeare
⚘
JOHANN GOTTFRIED HERDER

Editor's Notes

Index

Introduction

Herder's *Shakespeare* is a milestone in the development of literary theory. First published in 1773, as one of five contributions to a pamphlet edited by Herder himself and entitled *Von deutscher Art und Kunst* (On German Character and Art), it represents a defiant rejection of Enlightenment poetics, neoclassicism, and the dominance of French taste. It pioneers a new historicist, proto-Romantic approach to cultures and their products, one that favors the local over the universal, the authentic over the ersatz, the primitive over the modern.

It is a key document in the German reception of Shakespeare. And, perhaps most important of all, as the cornerstone of what has come to be seen as the manifesto of the Sturm und Drang movement, it exerted an unrivaled influence on the German literary renaissance of the 1770s.

The title of *Von deutscher Art und Kunst* clearly signals Herder's intention for the various essays to be seen as exploring different aspects of German cultural identity. It is rather less obvious, though, what Shakespeare has to do with any of this. In fact, most of the other pieces in the collection would not seem to be directly concerned with German culture in the narrow sense either, dealing as they do with Gothic architecture or with Ossian, the legendary Scottish bard who was enjoying a voguish prominence at the time thanks to the forgeries of James Macpherson. Only the extract from Justus Möser's patriotic *Osnabrück History* appears at all relevant. So what exactly is Herder driving at?

In the late eighteenth century Germany was little more than a vague geographical expression. It consisted of hundreds of autonomous territories, ranging in size from Lilliputian statelets to great powers such as Prussia and Austria, all nominally under the jurisdiction of the Holy Roman Empire of the German Nation. In this empire-on-paper—which lacked political, religious, and economic cohesion, and was ruled by a self-interested and Francophile elite—a unified national culture had failed to emerge. "We are laboring in Germany as in the days of the confusion of Babel," Herder once grumbled, "divided by sects of taste, partisans of poetic art, schools of philosophy contesting one another: no capital and no common interest, no great and universal reformer and lawgiving genius."[1] Intellectuals throughout the Germanies, Herder among them, felt acutely the absence of a public sphere and worked actively to create the conditions for a literary revival. For Herder that meant restoring continuities in German history and society; it meant renewing shared traditions that had been neglected, interrupted, extinguished, or buried beneath a superficial and alien civilization. Hence his deliberately capacious

---

[1] "Fragments: First Collection," in *Johann Gottfried Herder: Selected Early Works, 1764–1767*, ed. Ernest A. Menze and Karl Menges (University Park, PA: Pennsylvania State University Press, 1992), p. 95.

understanding of the term *deutsch*. He
takes it to signify not only the modern in-
habitants of the German-speaking lands
but those of Scandinavia and the British
Isles also, thereby opening up the old fault
line dividing Latin from Germanic Europe, the earthy, robust Teutons from the
decadent, effete *Welschen*. Moreover, he
uses the word in its original sense, as refer-
ring specifically to the language and art of
the people—unruly, coarse, yet creative—rather than those of the Ruritanian
ruling caste: urbane, polite, and sterile.
Herder's pamphlet is accordingly concerned with the ways in which these de-
motic energies might revitalize a mori-
bund culture from below.

A dose of Shakespeare was just the
tonic that German literature needed.
Herder was by no means alone in thinking

so. Ever since, if not before, Kaspar Wilhelm von Borck's translation of *Julius Caesar* in 1741, the first rendering of a complete Shakespeare play into German, the English dramatist had come to represent for German writers a welcome counterforce to the canons of French neoclassicism, a role that he had already fulfilled for Addison and others in Britain. Some saw him as a threat for that very reason. Johann Christoph Gottsched, who in the 1730s and 1740s was the most visible champion of French neoclassical drama as a template for German literature, was content to echo the complaints of Voltaire. In the eighteenth of his *Philosophic Letters* (1733), Voltaire had asserted with typical hauteur that, for all his forceful and fecund imagination, Shakespeare worked "without the least glimmer of good taste and without the least knowledge of the rules," and ended up producing "monstrous farces" instead of tragedies. Reviewing Borck's translation, Gottsched agreed. Borck had in fact squeezed Shakespeare into the corset of classical hexameters and, as was common practice in the eighteenth century, primped, pruned, and powdered the Elizabethan in an effort to make him presentable. But that did not prevent Gottsched from sniffily declaring that even the traditional vulgar spectacles he had spent his career attempting to banish from the German repertory were not so "full of blunders and faults in violation of the rules of the stage and good sense" as was Shakespeare.

Others were more enthusiastic—or at least less dismissive. That same year, Johann Elias Schlegel defended the bold strokes with which Shakespeare portrayed his characters. Yet Schlegel was unable wholly to free himself from the decorum of his time when criticizing Shakespeare's bawdy language and—a common reproach in the eighteenth century—the exuberance of his metaphor. Friedrich Nicolai, in his explicitly anti-Gottschedian polemic *Letters on the Current State of Belles Lettres in Germany* (1755), similarly thought, despite his reservations about Shakespeare's disorderliness, that the Englishman crafted formidable, many-sided characters who could act as a stimulus for German theater. Some years later, Lessing, Nicolai's coconspirator against Gottsched's creaking authority, agreed that Shakespeare would be a better example for his countrymen than Racine or

Corneille. In the famous seventeenth of the *Letters Concerning Recent Literature* (1759), he claimed that the terrible sublimity and melancholy of English drama were more congenial to the German temperament than were the *délicatesse* and *raffinement* of the French. More important, Lessing was unconvinced that Shakespeare's practice existed beyond the critical pale. In fact, the Englishman, in spite of his irregularities, achieved, and with greater success than Corneille, the same tragic purpose at which Sophocles aimed: the arousal of fear and pity. Lessing, then, views Shakespeare not as a rebel but as a supreme poet who ultimately, if unconsciously, is a profoundly Aristotelian dramatist, even though, or precisely because, he ignores the rigid and straitening conventions of French pseudoclassicism. Lastly, Herder's immediate precursor was Heinrich von Gerstenberg, who, in his *Letters on Curiosities of Literature* (1768), was the first German commentator to declare Shakespeare sui generis and so exempt his practice from the standards of the classical tradition. Whereas the object of Greek drama was the stirring of passions in the audience, Gerstenberg argued, Shakespeare strove to paint "living pictures of moral Nature." His works are not tragedies but "character pieces" that disclose, in every nuance and detail, the innermost thoughts and feelings of his heroes. Yet despite his promising and historically oriented starting point, Gerstenberg soon loses himself in inconsistencies and is ultimately unable to escape the pull of the ancients entirely.

But none of these writers, Herder thought, had done justice to Shakespeare's achievements or quite put their finger on why he was so uniquely significant a phenomenon.

Herder had first become acquainted with Shakespeare in 1764, under the tutelage of his friend, the philosopher Johann Georg Hamann. Over the next few years, he gave himself over to what he called his "frenzy" for the English poet. Not one to keep his enthusiasms to himself, he took every opportunity to share his discovery with others—with his new friend Goethe, most momentously, but also with his fiancée, Caroline Flachsland. Shakespeare was his "hobbyhorse," he confessed to her late in 1770, introducing the man who, as the correspondence during their courtship attests, would become the third apex in a long-running love triangle: "I have not so much read as *studied* him, and I underline the word; each of his plays is a complete philosophy of the passion whereof it treats."[2] Like many in Germany, Herder was reliant on Christoph Martin Wieland's idiosyncratic but nevertheless extremely influential prose translations of twenty-two Shakespearean dramas, published between 1762 and 1766. Though he thought little of Wieland's efforts, it struck Herder, as it had Lessing and Gerstenberg, that the rude vigor of Shakespeare's verse was a world away from the mannered artifice of French literature or its anemic

[2] Herder, *Briefe*, ed. Wilhelm Dobbek and Günter Arnold (Weimar: Böhlaus Nachfolger, 1977–2004), 1:277, 270–71.

German imitations. Already in 1768, in a review of J. J. Dusch's *Letters on the Cultivation of Taste* (1767), he described Shakespeare as "a genius with an imagination that always aims at grandeur, that can devise a plan, the very sight of which makes us giddy: a genius who is nothing in the individual embellishments but everything in the great, wild structure of the plot: a genius who, if he shall define the concept of the poet, must cause all didactic rhymesters, all wits to tremble."[3] Like Homer, like the prophets of the Old Testament, like Ossian, Shakespeare possessed an expressive power, a sensuous directness that was typical of what Herder called

[3] Herder, *Sämtliche Werke*, ed. Bernhard Suphan (Berlin: Weidmann, 1877–1913), 4:284.

"popular poetry" (*Volkspoesie*). If poetry was indeed, as he frequently asserted (borrowing a phrase of Hamann's), the "mother tongue of mankind," then these "primitive" figures spoke it with an easy fluency long since lost in the stilted, prosy world of the Enlightenment. Active when their respective national cultures were still unformed, they drew from the subterranean reservoirs of human imagination and feeling. They could, therefore, serve as models to regenerate German letters—if only it were possible to tap the same source of creativity.

These intuitions were by no means uncommon in the eighteenth century. Like that of many of his young compatriots, Gerstenberg foremost among them, Herder's response to Shakespeare owed a great deal to Edward Young's *Conjectures on Original Composition* (1759), which appeared in two separate German translations in 1760. Young's work did much to popularize in Germany the new artistic concept of genius, which had become fundamental to French and especially British critical discourse during the early and mid-eighteenth century. For Young (and for Shaftesbury) the genius was a second Creator, a Promethean figure who imitated not the ancients or other writers but only nature. Instead of taking his lead from elegant learning, the genius created instinctively, promiscuously, with God-given powers. His activity was not mechanical and deliberate but organic and effortless: "An *Original* may be said to be of a *vegetable* nature; it rises spontaneously from the vital root of Genius; it *grows*, it is not *made*." Inevitably, Shakespeare was for Young—as he was already for Joseph Addison—the prototype of an original genius who had no call for the rules of neoclassicism (which, "like Crutches, are a needful aid to the lame, tho' an impediment to the strong"), and it was as such that through Young's mediation he came to be regarded by the new generation of German bardolaters, who conveniently overlooked, in their eagerness to embrace Shakespeare as a primal force of nature, the rhetorical contrivances and sophistication of the Elizabethan dramatist.

These debates form the invisible backdrop to Herder's essay. We need to bear them in mind because Herder was a lifelong controversialist. His first major works, *On Recent German Literature: Fragments*, *Critical Forests*, *On the Origin of Language*, *Yet Another Philosophy of History*, and, toward the end of his life, *Kalligone* and the *Metacritique* began as ripostes to other writers and thinkers (the latter two are directed at Kant). Like a barroom bruiser, he was always spoiling for a fight, perpetually in need of an antagonist, a foil to help him articulate his own ideas. That is no less true of the essay at hand. Here, however, he is more reluctant than usual to single anyone out. Although he does explicitly take issue with Gerstenberg, as well as making approving noises about Lessing, his strategy is to mention the proliferation of critical literature only to reject it outright. The dispute between Shakespeare's champions and detractors is flawed because, irrespective of whether they heap praise or mockery on him, both parties take as their starting point and criteria for judging him the very conventions that Shakespeare quite evidently disregards. Instead, Herder wants to show *why* Shakespeare could not be bound by neoclassical rules and hence *why* he can serve as a new, freer model for modern European drama. Herder seeks to account for Shakespeare, to understand him, to enter into emotional dialogue with him, and thereby to "bring him to life for us Germans."

This is possible, he insists, only through a proper appreciation of the historical and cultural context within which art and genius emerge. Though poetic inspiration is universal, the manner in which it is expressed is not. Examining ancient Greek tragedy (as typified by Sophocles) and the modern northern European drama of Shakespeare, Herder shows that each arose under vastly different environmental conditions and from different antecedents; because each was shaped by different social, political, and material forces, they could not but be different and guided by different rules. They are thus two wholly distinct species of drama that, at least from one point of view, do not admit of comparison. Greek tragedy evolved (it was never static or monolithic) from the preexisting dithyramb and chorus, taking as its subject matter simple mythical events whose scope and expressive potential were increased as actors and scenes were gradually introduced. The classical unities of time, place, and plot, which Aristotle discovered inductively rather than arrived at a priori, were no arbitrary imposition on the creative artist; they were an entirely natural and necessary product of the simplicity of Greek life and customs: the "husk" within which the "fruit"—the individual artistic object—could grow. To attempt to replicate Sophoclean tragedy, or to apply its rules, in the entirely different milieu of seventeenth- and eighteenth-century France amounted to a refusal to acknowledge the historical and cultural specificity of Greek drama, and as such was not only absurd but positively harmful. The plays of Corneille, Racine, and Voltaire are true neither to their own age nor to that of the Greeks from which they purport to derive their legitimacy; they are but a decorous and flimsy parody, an empty shell lacking the soul, the living spirit, of the original. The identity of form and content has been violated. (The same criticism would hold true for German philhellenism, made fashionable by Winckelmann and eventually culminating in—as Herder later saw it—the travesties of Weimar Classicism.)

Shakespeare, by contrast, reflects his own historical reality. The greater complexity and diversity of social life in early modernity are manifested in the sheer variety of events, localities, and characters in his plays, precisely those features that seemed to men like Gottsched to offend against the proprieties of dramatic art.[4]

---

[4] Samuel Johnson in 1765, in the preface to his edition of Shakespeare, which was translated and used by Wieland also, similarly argues that the mingling of tragedy and comedy, the interplay of moods, and the utter range of characters constituted the

His scenes are not stylized fictions like those of the French: we are confronted with nature in all its concrete and tumultuous immediacy. Because Shakespeare did not, like the Greeks, live in an age characterized by unity, such unity could not arise of itself in his dramas. Hence in order to transform the disparate stuff of his age into a whole, into a single work of art, his approach had to be the opposite of Sophocles'. Where the drama of the ancients became more intricate over time—within self-imposed constraints—Shakespeare, as the exemplary modern poet, creates uniformity out of multiplicity. He cannot very well put the entire world on the stage, so he must compress it into a

---

quintessence of Shakespeare's genius; but Herder is the first to explain why that is the case.

single, awesome event. But the unity he arrives at is purely ideal, the necessary means by which he is able to bring forth a self-sustaining aesthetic illusion. It has nothing to do with the dictates of neoclassicism, and ultimately depends on the power of the poet to transcend our categories of perception and insist on his own measure of time and space. Even where Shakespeare seems to take too many liberties, with his telescoping of time and abrupt accelerations of action, it turns out that he is being faithful to ordinary human experience. Time and space, as Herder reminds us, are not absolute. The internal clock ticking as the drama unfolds may not be synchronized with the watches we wear as we sit in the playhouse—but Shakespeare is able thereby to convey a deeper psychological truth.

So where Sophoclean tragedy, born of myth, remained abstract and universal, Shakespeare's theater, the roots of which lie in the popular carnival plays of the Renaissance, discloses his turbulent world in all its vibrancy and individuality and disparity. But although Sophocles and Shakespeare may be outwardly dissimilar, they have a spiritual kinship that all geniuses share: they are true not only to nature (as Young argued) but also to the culture from which they emerged (and herein lies Herder's decisive contribution to the concept of genius). Both are mouthpieces of the collective soul of the nation, expressing its thoughts and sentiments, manners and morals; in each case their art is a development of indigenous species of expression. Though their purpose—the manufacture of theatrical illusion, the convulsion of the heart—is the same, their means are necessarily different.[5] Nevertheless, each dramatic form has its own legitimacy, and—this is Herder's point—so might any other literature that is unfettered and faithful to its national character.

But there is more. In his important treatise *Yet Another Philosophy of History*—a sardonic reply to the Enlightenment's complacent ideology of progress, published in 1774—Herder views history as an apparently aimless chain of events whose plan is inscrutable and known only to God. He repeatedly compares history to a

---

[5] Whilst Herder claims that Sophoclean and Shakespearean drama are more or less entirely different phenomena, this is true only of their form: the essence or purpose of drama would appear to have remained unchanged over time.

mighty drama in which props and players are moved about on a cosmic stage so that the Divine Author's purpose may be achieved, even if the actors are only dimly aware of the greater scheme of things. *Shakespeare*, completed a year earlier, is clearly a stepping-stone toward the understanding of historical processes advanced there. But here the analogy is reversed: Shakespeare dramatizes history, but not just in the ordinary sense of writing historical plays. So overwhelmed are we when reading him that we forget this is a mere text subject to the restraints and confines of the theater. (And it is surely important to bear in mind that Herder speaks of the experience of *reading* Shakespeare, not of witnessing an actual performance: few Shakespeare plays had been staged in Germany at the time of his writing.) Shakespeare's plays *are* history itself; or at least the vehicle through which history comes alive. The poet is a creator in miniature, an intermediary between God and the world, whose work is akin to Revelation. So complete is the illusion of his richly imagined universe, with its own dimensions, its own beginning and end, a microcosm into which so many fragments of human experience and passion have been intruded, that we feel we are powerless, a blind tool of his will, just like the characters we see hastening toward their fall. Yet at the same time we sense the identity of Shakespeare's dramatic procedure and the logic of history: he reproduces its modes of operation in the apparent chaos and confusion we see unfold before us. As in life, we cannot clearly discern the larger design; but Shakespeare nevertheless gives us an inkling of it, enabling us to glimpse "dark little symbols forming the silhouette of a divine theodicy." And what we glimpse are the lineaments of Spinoza's God, *natura naturans*, an unending process of being, destructive yet self-renewing. *Shakespeare*, then, is not just—perhaps not even primarily—literary criticism: the justification of God is at the heart of Herder's project.

Shakespeare is typical of Herder's style: impetuous, exuberant, exclamatory; suggestive but never conclusive. It is a way of writing that is deliberately opposed to the Enlightenment ideals of sobriety, balance, objectivity, and reasonableness. A theorist suspicious of theories, an avowed enemy of abstraction, Herder tried to achieve the same immediacy and spontaneity in his work that characterized the expression of earlier epochs, to overcome what Schiller called the "sentimental" mode of consciousness by assuming—ironically enough—a calculated naïveté, an artful artlessness. If Shakespeare is the new Sophocles, then Herder, by implication, must be the new Aristotle, seeking a kind of criticism commensurate with its subject, one that is itself "Shakespearean" in language and tone. By preferring to "rhapsodize" rather than analyze—for example, in his breathless summaries of *Othello*, *Macbeth*, *Hamlet*, and *King Lear*—Herder hopes to effect the empathetic understanding that will "bring Shakespeare to life." As a result, his exegetical interest in Shakespeare is necessarily limited and diverges from that of contemporary and later Romantic commentators. He does not deduce a moral system from the plays as a whole. He is unconcerned with character or form, with the literary or dramatic qualities of the plays. He is indifferent to antiquarian detail or textual subtleties. Characteristic, too, is the way the discussion breaks off just as it seems to get going, when Herder remarks offhandedly that "at this point the heart of my inquiry might begin." But even this is a device. Actually he has realized his primary objective, namely, to justify Shakespeare on historical grounds. Important though the present task is, Herder feels compelled to underline that it should be seen only as a first step, not as an end in itself. The further problems it raises promise to be even more consequential: for example, the question of the alchemy by which Shakespeare was able to "transform some worthless romance, tale, or fabulous history into such a living whole"—or in other words, the laws governing the agency of artistic genius. As Herder makes clear, an investigation of the relationship between individual poetic creativity and the legacy of tradition would not only have implications for the theory and practice of literature, but would also enrich our knowledge of history and philosophy. He gestures at a potentially vast terrain, one encompassing psychology, anthropology, and ethnology: an undiscovered country that he must perforce leave untrodden for the time being, but had begun to chart elsewhere and bring under the banner of "aesthetics." Once Herder has opened up this vista, it seems almost comically inadequate to go no further than the fish-in-a-barrel dismissal of Gerstenberg and his attempt to apply Polonius's system of classification to Shakespeare's dramas. But Herder does touch on these larger questions in his final remarks.

Herder's criticism not only strives to be sensitive to the historical circumstances of a work's origin but is also acutely aware of its own rootedness in a particular place and time: he can rhapsodize about Shakespeare precisely because Shakespeare speaks to that moment. But not for long. The essay's coda sees an abrupt shift from major to minor, from rapture to lament, with Herder complaining that his will be the last generation truly able to understand

Shakespeare. Already the Elizabethan age is becoming increasingly remote, the work itself destined to lose its vitality and become an incomprehensible object of wonder, as strange and exotic as the ruins of ancient Greece or Egypt. Even the "great creator of history" cannot in the end escape the inevitability of historical change. His world is no longer ours.

But surely this is an exaggeration? After all, *The Iliad* is a product of its age, in its concerns and characters and form; yet it is still read, and appreciated, thousands of years after its composition. In fact, Homer is an excellent example of what Herder is here gesturing toward. Long neglected in favor of the more "classical" and "tasteful" Virgil, Homer had been rediscovered in the eighteenth century and lived on in the translation of Pope, for example, whose achievement Herder admired and desired to see emulated in Germany. Ossian, too, had been resurrected, though in more problematical fashion by James Macpherson. Truly great poetry does indeed transcend its historicity. But it can do so only if it is constantly reinterpreted, reinvented, reinvigorated. Even Shakespeare will slip into oblivion unless writers actively engage with the past, but in such a way that the result is always provisional, temporary, surpassable, never absolute. Just as Shakespeare built on what went before him, so we must build on Shakespeare: he is now part of that long, continuous tradition that we must adapt and shape for our own ends. The important thing is not to imitate Shakespeare directly, but to follow his example: to be true to one's historical and cultural identity. Hence Herder's own translations of various scenes from the Shakespearean canon, in which he attempts to capture the essential otherness of the archaic and densely allusive English, pushing at the limits of what is possible in German prosody. Hence, too, his concluding apostrophe to Goethe, the friend whom he claims to have embraced before Shakespeare's "sacred image." Goethe's first major success, the Shakespeare-inspired drama *Götz von Berlichingen* (1773), put Herder's ideas into action and heralded a new literature based on native traditions and forms. But that is not all. Goethe takes as his subject history itself: the iron-handed Götz is a late-medieval knight struggling vainly against his own obsolescence, caught as he is on the cusp of transition from heroic individualism to the legal framework of modern civil society. Moreover, by setting his play in Germany's own "age of chivalry," as Herder demands, Goethe enacts the very essence of poetic practice: revisiting the past. Götz von Berlichingen, then, like Shakespeare, is not just an end but also a beginning.

Shakespeare

If any man brings to mind that tremendous image of one "seated high atop some craggy eminence, whirlwinds, tempest, and the roaring sea at his feet, but with the flashing skies about his head," that man is Shakespeare! Only we might add that below him, at the very base of his rocky throne, there murmur the multitudes who explain, defend, condemn, excuse, worship, slander, translate, and traduce him— and all of whom he cannot hear!

What a library has already been written about, for, and against him! And I have no mind to add to it in any way. It is my wish instead that no one in the small circle of those who read these pages would ever again think to write about, for, or against him, either to excuse or to slander him; but that they explain him, feel him as he is, use him, and—where possible—bring him to life for us Germans. If only this essay can help in some small way to realize this goal!

Shakespeare's boldest enemies—in how many different guises—have accused and mocked him, claiming that though he may be a great poet, he is not a good dramatist; or if he is a good dramatist, then he is not a classical tragedian equal in rank to men such as Sophocles, Euripides, Corneille, and Voltaire, who raised this art to the highest pinnacle of perfection. And

Shakespeare's boldest friends have mostly been content to *excuse*, to *defend* him from such attacks; to weigh his beauties against his transgressions of the rules and see the former as compensation for the latter; to utter the *absolvo* over the accused; and then to deify his greatness all the more immoderately, the more they were compelled to shrug their shoulders at his faults. That is how things stand even with the most recent editors and commentators— my hope is that these pages can change the prevailing point of view so that our image of him may emerge into a fuller light.

But is this hope not too bold? Too presumptuous, when so many great men have already written about him? I think not. If I can show that both sides have built their case merely on *prejudice*, on an illusion that does not really exist; if, therefore, I have merely to dispel a cloud from their eyes or at most adjust the image without in the least altering anything in eye or image, then perhaps it is down to my time or even to chance that I should have discovered the spot where I now detain the reader: "Stand here, otherwise you will see nothing but caricature!" If all we ever did was wind and unwind the tangled threads of learning without ever getting any further—then what an unhappy fate we would weave!

It is from Greece that we have inherited the words *drama*, *tragedy*, and *comedy*; and just as the lettered culture of the human race has, on a narrow strip of the earth's surface, made its way only through *tradi-*

tion, so a certain stock of rules, which seemed inseparable from its teaching, has naturally accompanied it everywhere in its womb and its language. Since a child cannot be and is not educated by means of reason but by means of authority, impression, and the divinity of example and of habit, so entire nations are to an even greater extent children in everything that they learn. The kernel would not grow without the husk, and they will never get the kernel without the husk, even if they could find no use for the latter. That is the case with Greek and northern drama.

In Greece the drama developed in a way that it could not in the north. In Greece it was what it can never be in the north. In the north it is not and cannot be what it was in Greece. Thus Sophocles' drama and Shakespeare's drama are two things that in a certain respect have scarcely their name in common. I believe I can demonstrate these propositions from Greece itself and in doing so decipher a great deal of the nature of the northern drama and of the greatest northern dramatist, Shakespeare. We shall observe the genesis of the one by means of the other, but at the same time see it transformed, so that it does not remain the same thing at all.

Greek tragedy developed, as it were, out of a single scene, out of the impromptu dithyramb, the mimed dance, the *chorus*. This was enlarged, recast: Aeschylus put two actors onto the stage instead of one, invented the concept of the protagonist, and reduced the choral part. Sophocles added a third actor and introduced scene painting—from such origins, though belatedly, Greek tragedy rose to greatness, became a masterpiece of the human spirit, the summit of poetry, which Aristotle esteems so highly and we, in Sophocles and Euripides, cannot admire deeply enough.

At the same time, however, we see that certain things can be explained in terms of these origins, which, were we to regard them as dead rules, we would be bound to misconstrue dreadfully. That *simplicity of the Greek plot*, that *sobriety of Greek manners*, that sustained, buskined style *of expression, song making, spectacle, unity of time and place*—all these things lay so naturally and inherently, without any artifice and magic, in the origins of Greek tragedy that it was made possible only as a consequence of their refinement. They were the husk in which the fruit grew.

Step back into the infancy of that age: *simplicity of plot* really was so steeped in what was called the *deeds of olden times*, in *republican, patriotic, religious, heroic action*, that the poet had more trouble distinguishing parts in this simple whole, introducing a dramatic beginning, middle, and end, than in forcibly separating them, truncating them, or kneading them into a whole out of many discrete events. This ought to be perfectly understandable to anyone who has read Aeschylus or Sophocles. In Aeschylus, what is tragedy often but *an allegorical, mythological, semiepic painting*, almost without a succession of scenes, story, sensations? Or is it not even, as the

8

ancients said, nothing but *chorus* into which a certain amount of story has been squeezed? Did the simplicity of his plots demand the least effort and art? And was it any different in the majority of Sophocles' plays? His *Philoctetes*, *Ajax*, *Oedipus Coloneus*, and so on, are still very close to the uniformity of their origin, the *dramatic picture framed by the chorus*. No doubt about it! This is the genesis of Greek drama!

Now let us see how much follows from this simple observation. Nothing less than this: "the artificiality of the rules of Greek drama was—not artifice at all! It was Nature!" Unity of plot—was the unity of the action that lay before the *Greeks*; which according to the circumstances of their time, country, religion, and manners could be nothing but this oneness. *Unity of place* was just that, unity of place; for the one brief, solemn action occurred only in a single locality, in the temple, in the palace, as it were in the market square of the nation; to begin with, this action was only mimed and narrated and interposed; then finally the entrances of the characters, the scenes were added—but of course it was all still but one scene, where the chorus bound everything together, where in the nature of things the stage could never remain empty, and so on. And even a child could see that unity of time now ensued from and naturally accompanied all this. In those days all these things lay in *Nature*, so that the poet, for all his art, could achieve nothing without them!

It is also evident that the art of the Greek poets took the very opposite path to the one that we nowadays ascribe to them. They did not *simplify*, it seems to me, but rather *elaborated*: Aeschylus expanded the *chorus* and Sophocles enlarged upon Aeschylus, and we need only compare the most sophisticated plays of Sophocles and his great masterpiece *Oedipus in Thebes* with *Prometheus* or with accounts of the ancient *dithyramb* to see the astonishing artistry with which he successfully endowed his works. But his was never an art of making a simple plot out of a complex one, but rather of making a complex plot out of a simple one, a beautiful labyrinth of scenes. His greatest concern remained, at the most intricate point in the labyrinth, to foster in his audience the illusion of the earlier simplicity, to unwind the knot of their feelings so gently and gradually as to make them believe they had never lost it, the previous dithyrambic feeling. To this end he expanded each scene, retained the choruses, and turned them into staging posts for the action; their every word ensured that his audience never lost sight of the whole, kept them in expectation, in the illusion of development, of *familiarity with the action* (all of which the didactic Euripides, when the drama had scarcely reached maturity, promptly neglected to do!). In short, he gave action *grandeur* (something that has been terribly misunderstood).

It ought to be clear to anyone who reads him without prejudice and from the standpoint of his own time that this is the art which Aristotle values in Sophocles, that in everything he took almost the opposite view to the spin that modern times have chosen to put on him. The very fact that he let Thespis and Aeschylus alone and stuck to the *variety* of Sophocles' poetry; that he took precisely Sophocles' *innovation* as his point of departure and viewed it as the *essence* of this new poetic genre; that it became his dearest wish to develop a new Homer and to compare him favorably with the original; that he did not neglect even the slightest detail that could in performance lend support to his conception of the action possessing *magnitude and grandeur*—all this shows that the great man also philosophized in the grand style of his age, and that he bears no blame at all for the restrictive and infantile follies that have turned him into the paper scaffolding of our stage. In his excellent chapter on the nature of plot he evidently "knew and recognized no other rules than the gaze of the spectator, soul, illusion!" and expressly states that *limitations* of length, still less of kind or time or place of the structure, cannot be determined by any other rules. Oh, if Aristotle were alive today and could witness the false, preposterous application of his rules in dramas of a quite different kind! But let us keep to calm and dispassionate inquiry.

As everything in the world changes, so Nature, the true creator of Greek drama, was bound to change also. *The Greek worldview, manners,* the *state of the republics, the tradition of the heroic age, religion,* even *music, expression,* and *the degrees of illusion* changed. And so naturally enough the material for plots disappeared, too, as well as the opportunity to adapt it and the motive for doing so. To be sure, the poets could draw on older or foreign material and dress it up in the tried-and-tested manner, but that had no effect. Consequently it was devoid of soul. Consequently (why should we mince our words?) it was no longer the thing it once was. It was effigy, imitation, ape, statue, in which only the most devoted lover could still detect the demon that had once brought the statue to life. Let us immediately turn to the new Athenians of Europe (for the Romans were too stupid or too clever or too wild and immoderate to establish a completely Hellenizing theater), and the matter becomes, I think, quite clear.

There is no doubt that this effigy of Greek theater can scarcely be more perfectly conceived and realized than it has been in France. I am thinking not only of the so-called dramatic rules that have been attributed to dear old Aristotle: *the unity of time, place,* and *action, the connection of the scenes, the verisimilitude of the scenery,* and so on. The question I really want to ask is whether anything in the world possibly exceeds the sleek, classical thing that the Corneilles, Racines, and Voltaires have produced, the series of beautiful *scenes, dialogues, verses,* and *rhymes* with their *measure, decorum, brilliance.* Not only does the author of the present essay doubt it, but all the admirers of Voltaire and the French, particularly those noble Athenians themselves, will positively *deny* it—indeed, they have done so often enough already, they are still doing it, and they will continue to do so: "There is nothing better!

It cannot be surpassed!" And from the point of view of this outward conformity, with this effigy treading the boards, they are right and must daily be more so, the more every country in Europe is besotted with this slick superficiality and continues to ape it.

But for all that, there is still the oppressive, inescapable feeling that "this is no Greek tragedy! This is no Greek drama in its purpose, effect, kind, and nature!" And that even the most partisan admirer of the French cannot deny, once he has experienced the Greeks. I do not even propose to inquire "whether they observe their Aristotelian rules as scrupulously as they claim to, for Lessing has recently raised serious doubts about the pretensions they trumpet most loudly." But even if we admit that they do keep to these rules, French drama is still not the same thing as Greek drama. Why? Because nothing in their inner essence is the same—not action, manners, language, purpose, nothing. So what is the good of carefully preserved outward similarities? Does anyone really believe that a single one of the great Corneille's heroes is a Roman or French hero? They are Spanish-Senecan heroes! Gallant heroes; adventurous, brave, magnanimous, love-struck, cruel heroes, and therefore dramatic fictions who outside the theater would be branded fools and who even in those days, at least in France, were almost as outlandish as they are in most modern plays. Racine speaks the language of sentiment—granted, in this single instance of agreement he is unsur-

passed, but then again—I would not know
where sentiment ever spoke in such a way.
They are thirdhand pictures of sentiment;
they are never or only rarely the immediate, original, unadorned emotions, search-
ing for words and finding them at last.
Voltaire's beautiful verse, its arrangement,
content, economy of images, polish, wit,
philosophy—is it not beautiful verse? Indeed it is! The most beautiful that one can
imagine, and if I were a Frenchman, I
would despair at writing poetry after Voltaire—but beautiful or not, it is not theatrical verse appropriate to the action, language, manners, passions, and purpose of
a drama (other than the French kind); it is
never-ending rhetoric, lies, and galimatias!
And the ultimate *aim* of it all? It is certainly
not a Greek aim, a tragic purpose! To

stage a beautiful play, as long as it is also a beautiful action! To let a series of respectable, well-dressed ladies and gentlemen recite beautiful speeches and the most beautiful and useful philosophy in beautiful verse! And then to put them all in a story that produces the illusion of reality and thus captivates our attention! Finally, to have it all performed by a number of well-rehearsed ladies and gentlemen, who do their very best to win our applause and approval through declamation, stilted delivery of the sententious speeches, and the outward expression of emotions—all this might serve excellently as a living manual, an exercise in correct expression, in conduct and decorum, as a portrait of good or even heroic manners, and even as a complete academy of national wisdom and decency in matters of life and death (without taking into account all its subsidiary aims). Beautiful, formative, instructive, and excellent all this may be, but it shows neither hide nor hair of the purpose of Greek theater.

And what was this purpose? Aristotle has declared it to be—and there has been enough dispute about it ever since—no more nor less than a *certain* convulsion of the heart, the agitation of the soul to a *certain degree* and in *certain aspects*; in short, a *species of illusion* that surely no French play has ever achieved or ever will achieve. And consequently (no matter how lovely and useful the name that we give it) it is not Greek drama. It is not Sophoclean tragedy. It is an effigy outwardly resembling Greek drama; but the effigy lacks spirit, life, nature, truth—that is, all the elements that move us; that is, the tragic purpose and the accomplishment of that purpose. So can it still be the same thing?

This does not yet decide the value or otherwise of French drama but only raises the question of difference, which I believe my foregoing remarks to have put beyond doubt. I shall leave it to the reader to determine for himself "whether a half-truthful copying of foreign ages, manners, and actions, with the exquisite aim of adapting it to a two-hour performance on our stage, can be thought the equal or indeed the superior of an *imitation* that in a certain respect was the highest expression of a people's national character." I shall leave it to the reader to determine (and here every Frenchman will have to wriggle out of this difficulty or sing so tunelessly that he drowns out the reproaches of his critics) whether a poetic work that properly speaking has *no purpose at all* as a whole— for according to the testimony of the best philosophers its virtue lies only in the selection of detail—whether such a copy can be equal in value to a *national institution* whose every little particular produces an effect and betokens the highest, richest culture. Whether, finally, a time may come when, just as the greater part and most artificial of Corneille's plays are already forgotten today, Crébillon and Voltaire will be regarded with the same admiration that we now reserve for the *Astrea* of d'Urfé and all the *Clélie*s and *Aspasia*s from the age of chivalry: "How clever, wise, inventive, and well-crafted they are! There would be so much to learn from them, but what a pity it is to be found in the *Astrea* and *Clélie*." Their whole art is unnatural, fanciful, dainty! How fortunate if that time had already arrived for our taste for truth! The whole of French drama would have transformed itself into a collection of beautiful verses, sententiousness, and sentiments—but the great *Sophocles will still stand where he is today!*

So let us now suppose a nation, which due to particular circumstances that will not detain us here, did not care to ape the Greeks and settle for the mere walnut shell, but preferred instead to *invent its own drama.* Then, it seems to me, our first questions must once again be: *When? Where?* Under *what conditions? Out of which materials should it do so?* And no proof is needed that this invention can and will be the result of these questions. If this people does not develop its drama out of the chorus and dithyramb, then it can have no choral or dithyrambic parts. If its *history, tradition,* and *domestic, political, and religious relations* have no such simple character, then naturally its drama cannot partake of this quality either. Where possible, it will *create* its drama out of its history, out of the spirit of the age, manners, opinions, language, national prejudices, traditions, and pastimes, even out of carnival plays and puppet plays (just as the noble Greeks did from the chorus). And what it creates will be drama if it achieves its dramatic purpose among this people. As the reader will see, we have arrived among the *toto divisis ab orbe Britannis* and their great Shakespeare.

That this was not Greece, neither in Shakespeare's day nor earlier, no *pullulus Aristotelis* will deny, and therefore to demand that Greek drama arise then, and in England, to demand that it develop *naturally* (we are not speaking here of mere apery) is worse than asking a sheep to give birth to lion cubs. Our first and last question is simply this: "What is the soil like? How has it been prepared? What has been sown in it? What should it be able to produce?" And heavens, how far we are from Greece! History, tradition, manners, religion, the spirit of the age, of the people, of emotion, and of language—how far all these things are from Greece! Whether the reader knows both ages well or only slightly, he will not for one moment confuse two things that bear no likeness to each other. And if now in this changed

time, changed for good or ill, there arose
an age, a genius who created dramatic
works from this raw material as naturally,
sublimely, and originally as the Greeks did
from theirs; and if these works reached the
same goal by very different paths; and if
they were essentially a far more multi-
formly simple and uniformly complex en-
tity, and thus (according to all metaphysi-
cal definitions) a perfect whole—what
manner of fool would now compare and
even condemn the two things because the
latter was not the former? Indeed, the very
essence, virtue, and perfection of the latter
reside in the fact that it is not the former,
that from the soil of the age a different
plant grew.

Shakespeare was confronted with
nothing like the simplicity of national
manners, deeds, inclinations, and histori-

cal traditions that formed the Greek drama. And since, according to the first principle of metaphysics, nothing comes from nothing, then, if it were left to philosophers, not only would there have been no Greek drama but if nothing else existed besides, no drama at all anywhere in the world would subsequently have developed or could ever develop. But since it is known that genius is more than philosophy and a creator wholly distinct from an analyzer, so a mortal was endowed with divine powers to summon from completely different material and by quite different means precisely the same effect, *fear* and *pity*, and to a degree of which the earlier treatment and material were scarcely capable. Oh, happy was this son of the gods in his undertaking! The very innovativeness, originality, and variety of his work demonstrate the primal power of his vocation.

Shakespeare had no chorus before him; but he did have historical dramas and puppet plays—well then! So from these historical dramas and puppet plays, from this inferior clay, he fashioned the glorious creation that stands before us and lives! He found nothing comparable to the simple character of the Greek people and their polity, but rather a rich variety of different estates, ways of life, convictions, peoples, and idioms—any nostalgia for the simplicity of former times would have been in vain. He therefore brought together the estates and individuals, the peoples and idioms, the kings and fools, fools and kings, to form one glorious whole! He found no such simple spirit of history, plot, and action; he took history as he found it, and with his creative spirit he combined the most diverse material into a wondrous whole, which, if we cannot call *plot* as the Greeks understood the word, we shall describe as *action* in the medieval sense, or what in the modern age is termed *event* (*événement*), great *occurrence*. O Aristotle, if you were alive today, what comparisons you would draw between the modern Sophocles and Homer! You would devise a theory that would do justice to him, the like of which even his own countrymen Home and Hurd, Pope and Johnson have yet to come up with! You would be glad to trace the trajectory of *plot*, *character*, *thought*, *language*, *song making*, and *spectacle* from each of your plays, as though you were drawing lines from two points at the base of a triangle so that they converge at the point where they complete the figure, the point of *perfection*! You would say to Sophocles: "Paint the sacred panels of this altar! And you, O northern bard, cover every side and every wall of this temple with your immortal fresco!"

Let me continue as expounder and rhapsodist, for I am closer to Shakespeare than to the Greek. If in Sophocles a single *action* prevails, then Shakespeare aims at the totality of an *event*, an *occurrence*. If in Sophocles' characters a *single tone* predominates, then Shakespeare assembles all the characters, estates, and ways of life that are necessary to produce the main melody of his symphony. If in Sophocles *a single* refined and musical language resounds as if in some ethereal realm, then Shakespeare speaks the language of all ages, peoples, and races of men; he is the interpreter of Nature in all her tongues—and can both, though they travel so very different paths, be familiars of a single Divinity? And if Sophocles represents and teaches and moves and cultivates *Greeks*, then Shakespeare teaches, moves, and cultivates northern *men*! When I read him, it seems to me that the theater, actors, and scenery disappear! I see only separate leaves from the book of events, of Providence, of the world, blown by the storm of history; individual impressions of peoples, estates, souls, all the most various and independently acting machines, all the unwitting, blind instruments—which is precisely what we are in the hands of the Creator of the world—which come together to form a single, whole dramatic image, an event of singular grandeur that only the poet can survey. Who can conceive of a greater poet of northern man and of his age?

Step before his stage as before an ocean of events, where wave crashes into wave. Scenes from Nature come and go, each affecting the other, however disparate they appear to be; they are mutually creative and destructive, so that the intention of the creator, who seems to have combined them all according to a wanton and disordered plan, may be realized—dark little symbols forming the silhouette of a divine theodicy. Lear, the impetuous, fiery dotard, noble yet feeble as he stands before his map, giving away crowns and dividing up his country—the first scene already carries within it the seeds of his later fate, which shall be brought to harvest in the darkest future. Behold! We shall soon see the good-hearted squanderer, the rash and merciless ruler, the childish father even in the antechambers of his daughters—pleading, praying, begging, cursing, ranting, blessing, and—dear Lord!—foreknowing his own madness. Then we shall see him abroad with uncovered head in thunder and lightning, fallen among the lowest class of men, with a fool for company and squatting in the cave of a crazed beggar, almost calling down madness from the heavens. And now we see him as he is, in all the simple majesty of his wretchedness and abandonment; and now with his wits restored, illuminated by the last

34

ray of hope, only for it then to be extinguished forever, forever! Finally, imprisoned, with the child, the daughter who had comforted and forgiven him dead in his arms, he then dies over her body, and the old servant follows the old king into death—my God! What vicissitudes of times, circumstances, storms, weather, and ages. And all of it not merely a single story—a drama of state, if you will—moving from a single beginning to a single conclusion, in accordance with the strictest rule of your Aristotle; rather, come closer, and feel the *human spirit* that also arranged each person and age and character and secondary thing in the picture. Two old fathers and all their very different children! The son of the one suffers misfortune yet is grateful to his deceived father; the other enjoys abominably good fortune yet is terribly ungrateful to his good-hearted father. One father against his daughters and they against him, their husbands, suitors, and all their accomplices in fortune and misfortune. Blind Gloucester on the arm of the son he fails to recognize, and mad Lear at the feet of his exiled daughter! And now the moment at the crossroads of fortune, when Gloucester dies beneath his tree and the trumpet sounds, all the minor details, motives, characters, and situations condensed into the work—everything is in play, developing into a whole, arranged together to form a *whole* comprising *fathers*, *children*, *kings*, *fools*, *beggars*, and *misery*, yet throughout which the soul of the event breathes in even the most disparate

scenes, in which places, times, circumstances, even, I would say, the heathen *fa-
talism* and *astrology* that prevail throughout, are so much a part of this whole that
I could not change or move a thing, or
introduce into it elements from other
plays or vice versa. And this is not a drama?
And Shakespeare not a dramatic poet? He
who embraces a hundred scenes of a world
event in his arms, orders them with his
gaze, and breathes into them the one soul
that suffuses and animates everything; he
who captivates our attention, our heart,
our every passion, our entire soul from beginning to end?—if not more, then let Father Aristotle bear witness: "creatures and
other organic structures must have magnitude, and yet be easily taken in by the eye"
and here—good heavens!—how Shake-

speare feels the whole course of events in the depths of his soul and brings it to its conclusion! A world of dramatic history, as vast and profound as Nature; but it is the creator who gives us the eyes and the vantage point we need to see so widely and deeply!

In *Othello*, the Moor, what a world! What a whole! A *living history of the genesis, development, eruption, and sad end to the passion of this noble and unfortunate man*! And what complexity! All these different cogs turning within a single mechanism! How this Iago, the Devil in human form, must look on the world and toy with everyone around him! And how *this* particular grouping of *these* particular characters, Cassio and Roderigo, Othello and Desdemona, with their susceptibilities like tinder to his infernal flames, must stand around him; each of them is caught in his net, used by him, and everything hastens to its sad conclusion. If an angel of Providence were to weigh human passions against one another and assemble souls and characters accordingly, and gave them occasions for each to act in the illusion of free will, when all along he led them by this illusion as if tugging at the chain of fate—this is how the human mind devised, conceived, sketched, and guided the events of this work.

There should be no need to remind anyone that time and place always accompany action just as the husk always surrounds the kernel, and yet precisely this point has raised the loudest outcry. If Shakespeare had the divine knack of comprehending an entire world of the most disparate scenes as a single great event, then naturally it was part of the truth of his events to represent time and place ideally in each instance so that they also contributed to the illusion. Is there indeed anyone in the world who is indifferent to the time and place of even the most trifling incidents of his life? And are they not especially important in those situations where the entire soul is agitated, formed, and transformed—in youth, in scenes of passion, in all the actions that shape our lives? Is it not precisely time and place and the fullness of external circumstances that necessarily lend the whole story *substance*, *duration*, and *existence*? And can a child, a youth, a lover, a man in the field of action ever suffer the amputation of a single detail of his locality, of the how, where, and when, without injury to the larger mental picture we have formed of his soul? In this, Shakespeare is the greatest master, precisely because he is only and always the servant of Nature. When he conceived the events of his drama and revolved them in his mind, he also revolved times and places for each instance! Out of all the possible conjunctions of time and place, Shakespeare selects, as though by some law of fatality, the very ones that are the most powerful, the most appropriate for the feeling of the action; in which the strangest, boldest circumstances best support the illusion of truth, where the changes of time and place, over which the poet is master, cry out the loudest: "This is no poet, but a creator! This is a history of the world!"

For instance, when the poet turned over in his mind as a fact of creation the terrible regicide, the tragedy called *Mac-*

beth—if then, my dear reader, you were too timid to give yourself over to the feeling of setting and place in any scene, then woe betide Shakespeare and the withered page in your hand. For you felt nothing of the opening scene with the witches on the heath amid thunder and lightning, nothing when the bloody man brings news of Macbeth's deeds to the king, who sends word that he shall be rewarded with another title, not to mention when the scene abruptly shifts and Macbeth receives the witches' prophetic greeting, is then apprised of Duncan's intentions, and these tidings mingle in his mind! You did not see his wife stride through the castle clutching that fateful letter, who will later wander in a so very different and terrible manner! You did not enjoy with the un-

suspecting king the sweet evening air for
one last time, in this house where the
martlet makes its pendant bed so safely,
but you, O king—for unseen forces are at
work—you are nearing your murderous
grave. The house is in commotion, the
servants making ready for guests and
Macbeth for murder! Banquo's prepara-
tory night scene with torch and sword!
The dagger, the terrible vision of the
dagger! The bell—the deed has scarcely
been done and now there is knocking at
the door! The discovery, the assembled
household—consider every possible time
and place, and you will see that the dramatic intention of this work could not
have been realized other than *here* and *in
this manner*. The scene of Banquo's murder
in the wood; the evening banquet and

Banquo's ghost—then once again the blasted heath (for Macbeth's terrible, fateful deed has been done!). Now the witches' cavern, the necromancy, the prophecy, the rage and despair! The slaying of Macduff's children, with only their mother to protect them under her wing! And the two fugitives beneath the tree, and then the terrifying sleepwalker roaming through the castle, and the marvelous fulfillment of the prophecy—Birnam Wood drawing near—Macbeth's death by the sword of one not of woman born—I would have to list each and every scene if I wanted to give a name to the setting that is so perfectly in keeping with the spirit of this unnameable whole, *this world of fate, regicide, and magic* that is the soul of the play and breathes life into it right down to the smallest detail of time, place, and even the apparently haphazard episodes in between; I would have to list each and every scene in order to imagine them all as a single dreadful, indivisible whole—and yet for all that I would have said nothing.

The *individual quality* of each drama, of each separate universe, accompanies time and place and composition throughout all the plays. Lessing compared several features of *Hamlet* with the theatrical queen Semiramis—how the spirit of the place pervades the entire drama from beginning to end! The castle platform and the biting cold, the watch relieved and stories swapped in the night, disbelief and credulity, the star in the sky, and now the ghost appears! Is there anyone who does not sense art and Nature in every word and detail! And so it continues. All ghostly and human guises are exhausted! The cock crows and the drum sounds, the silent beckoning and the nearby hill, words natural and supernatural—what a setting! How deeply truth is embedded in it! And how the terrified king kneels, and Hamlet strays past his father's picture in his mother's chamber! And now the other scene! Hamlet at Ophelia's grave! The pathetic good fellow in all his dealings with Horatio, Ophelia, Laertes, Fortinbras! Hamlet's youthful toying with action, which runs throughout the play and does not become full action until almost the end—if there is anyone who for one moment feels and looks for the boards of the stage and a series of versified and elegant speeches on it, neither Shakespeare nor Sophocles nor indeed any true poet in the world has written for him.

If only I had the words to describe the one main feeling that prevails in each drama and courses through it like a world soul. As it does in *Othello*, where it is truly an essential element of the drama, as it does in the nocturnal search for Desdemona, their fabulous love, the voyage, the tempest, as it does in Othello's volatile passion, in the much-mocked manner of her death, disrobing as she sings her song of willow and the wind knocking; as in the nature of the sin and passion itself—Othello's entrance, his address to the candle, and so on—if only it were possible to capture all this in words, how it is all a vital and profound part of a single world, a single tragic event. But it is not possible.

Words cannot even describe or render the most wretched painted picture, so it is assuredly beyond their power to deliver the feeling of a single living world in all the scenes, circumstances, and enchantments of Nature. Examine whichever play you wish, dear reader, whether *Lear* or the *Richards*, *Julius Caesar* or the *Henrys*, even the supernatural plays and the *divertissements*, especially *Romeo and Juliet*, that sweet drama of love, a romance even in every detail of time and place and dream and poetry—examine the drama you have chosen and try to subtract something from its nature, to exchange it, or even to simplify it for the French stage—a living world in all the authenticity of its truth transformed into this wooden skeleton— a fair exchange, a fine transformation that

48

would be! Deprive this flower of its soil, its sap and vital force, and plant it in the air; deprive this person of place, time, individuality—and you have robbed him of breath and soul, leaving him nothing more than a *simulacrum of a living being*.

So Shakespeare is Sophocles' brother precisely where he seems so dissimilar, only to be inwardly wholly like *him*. Since all illusion is accomplished by means of this authenticity, truth, and creativity of history, then were they absent, not only would illusion be impossible, but not a single element of Shakespeare's drama and dramatic spirit would remain (or else I have written in vain). Thus we see that the whole world is merely the body belonging to this great spirit: all the scenes of Nature are the limbs of this body, just as every character and way of thinking is a feature of this spirit—and we might call the whole by the name of Spinoza's vast God: "Pan! Universum!" Sophocles remained true to Nature when he adapted a single action in a single time and place; Shakespeare could remain true to Nature only if he tossed his world events and human destinies through all the times and places in which—well, in which they occurred. And may God have mercy on the sportive Frenchman who arrives during Shakespeare's fifth act, thinking he will thereby be able to gulp down the quintessence of the play's feeling. That may be possible with some French dramas, because everything is versified and trotted out in scenes merely for theatrical effect; but with Shakespeare he would come away empty-handed. The world event would have already reached its conclusion; he would catch only its last and least consequence—that is, people dropping like flies—quit the playhouse, and sneer: Shakespeare is unto him a stumbling block and his drama the most half-witted foolishness.

The whole knot of questions concerning time and place would have been untangled long ago if a philosophical mind had taken the trouble to ask of the drama, "What do we mean by *time* and *place* anyway?" If the place is the stage and time the duration of a *divertissement au théâtre*, then the only people in the world to insist on the unities of place and time are the French. The Greeks, with a degree of illusion almost beyond our conception, whose stage was a public institution and was rightly regarded with religious devotion, never gave the unities a single thought. What manner of illusion is it when a person looks at his watch after every scene to ascertain whether such an action could have taken place in such and such a time, and whose heart's delight it then is that the poet has not swindled him of a single moment but has shown just as much on the stage as the spectator would see unfolding in the same time in the snail's pace of his own life—what kind of creature would derive from this his highest pleasure? And what kind of poet would view this as his main object, and then pride himself on this nonsense of rules, saying, "How many pretty trifles I have nicely crammed and fitted into the narrow space of this stage, called *théâtre Français*, and all in the prescribed time of a social visit; how I have threaded and spun the scenes! How carefully I have patched and stitched it all together!" What a wretched master of ceremonies! A Savoyard of the theater, not a creator, poet, or god of the drama! For if you are a true artist, no clock strikes on tower or temple for you, because you create your own space and time; and if you are able to create a world that cannot but exist in the categories of space and time, behold, your measure of space and duration is there within you, and you must enchant all your spectators so that they believe in it, you must obtrude it on them—or else you are, as I have said, anything but a dramatic poet.

Is there anyone in the world who requires proof that space and time are actually in themselves nothing, that in their connection to existence, action, passion, train of thought, and degree of attention within and without the soul, they are entirely relative? Were there never occasions in your life, good timekeeper of the drama, when hours seemed like moments and days like hours? Or conversely, when hours stretched into days and the night watch into years? Have you never known situations in your life when your soul sometimes dwelled wholly outside you? Here, in your beloved's romantic chamber; there, staring at that stiff corpse; here, in the oppression of external and humiliating distress—and then your soul took wing and soared beyond world and time, overleaping the spaces and regions of the earth, oblivious to everything around it, to reside in heaven, or in the soul, the heart of the one whose existence you now feel? And if that is possible in your sluggish and somnolent, wormish and vegetable life, where there are roots enough to hold you fast to the dead ground, and every circuit that you creep is measure enough for your snail's pace—then imagine yourself for a moment transported to another, poetic world, to a dream. Have you never felt how in dreams space and time disappear? How insubstantial they must be, mere shadows compared with *action*, with the working of the soul? How it is up to the soul to create its own space, world, and time, however and wherever it wishes? And if you had felt that only once in your life, if you had awoken after a mere quarter of an hour and the obscure remnants of your actions in the dream led you to swear that you had slept, dreamed, and acted for nights at a time, then Mahomet's dream would not for one moment seem absurd to you. And is it not the first and only duty of every genius, of every poet, and of the dramatic poet in particular, to remove you to such a dream? And now think what worlds you would confound if you were to show the poet your pocket watch or your drawing room so that he might teach you to dream according to their dictates.

The poet's space and time lie in the unfolding of his event, in the *ordine successivorum et simultaneorum* of *his* world. How and where does he transport you? As long as he transports you, you are in his world. However quickly or slowly he makes time pass, it is he who makes it pass; it is he who impresses its sequence on you: that is his measure of time—and what a master Shakespeare is in this respect, too! The events in his world begin as slowly and ponderously as they do in Nature herself, for it is Nature that he represents, only on a reduced scale. How laborious is the preparation before the machinery is set in motion; but once it gets going, how the scenes hurry past, how fleeting the speeches, how winged the souls, the passion, the action, and how powerful then this swift movement, the scattered delivery of individual words when time has run out for everyone. Finally, when the reader is entirely caught up in the illusion he has created, and is lost in the abyss of his world and his passion, how bold he becomes, what events he has succeed one another!

Lear dies after Cordelia, and Kent after Lear! It is the end of his world, as it were, as if the Day of Judgment had come, when everything, the Heavens included, collides and crashes, and the mountains fall; the measure of time is no more. But not for the merry *Cacklogallinian*, of course, who would arrive unharmed for the fifth act to measure with his watch how many died and how long it took. But dear God, if that is supposed to be criticism, theater, illusion—what might constitute criticism? or illusion? or theater? What do all these empty words signify?

At this point the heart of my inquiry might begin: "How, by what art and manner of creation, was Shakespeare able to transform some worthless romance, tale, or fabulous history into such a living whole? What laws of *historical, philosophical*, or *dramatic art* are revealed in every step he takes, in every device he employs?" What an inquiry that would be! How it would profit our historiography, our philosophy of the human soul, our drama! But I am not a member of all our academies of history and philosophy and the fine arts, where of course they devote their thoughts to anything but such a question! Even Shakespeare's countrymen do not consider it. What historical errors his commentators have often rebuked him for; what historical beauties have been censured—for example, in that hefty edition by Warburton! And did the author of the most recent essay on Shakespeare hit on my pet idea and ask, "how did Shakespeare compose drama from romances and tales?" It scarcely occurred to him, no more than it did to the Aristotle of this British Sophocles, Lord Home.

So just a nod in the direction of the usual classification of his plays. Just recently a writer who certainly has a deep feeling for Shakespeare had the idea of making that honest fishmonger of a courtier, with his gray beard and wrinkled face, his eyes purging thick amber and his *plentiful lack of wit together with weak hams*, of making the childish Polonius the poet's Aristotle, and proposed that the series of "-als" and "-cals" that this blatherer spouts should be taken seriously as the basis of classification for all of Shakespeare's plays.[1] I have my doubts. Shakespeare was admit-

[1] *Briefe über Merkwürdigkeiten der Litteratur. Dritte Sammlung.*

tedly cunning enough to put into the mouths of his characters, especially children and fools, the empty *locos communes*, morals, and classifications, which, when applied to a hundred cases, are appropriate to all and to none; and a new Stobaeus and *Florilegium*, or cornucopia of Shakespeare's wisdom, such as the English already possess and we Germans—may God be praised—are supposed to have had recently, would bring the greatest cheer to a Polonius, Lancelot, the *clowns* and *jesters*, poor Richard or the puffed-up *king of knights*, because every character of sound mind in Shakespeare never speaks more than is necessary for the action. But even here I still have my doubts. Polonius is here meant to be the great baby who takes clouds for camels and camels for bass viols,

who in his youth once played Julius Caesar, and was accounted a good actor and
was killed by Brutus and knows very well
"why day is day, night night and time is
time"—that is, here too he is spinning a
top of theatrical words. But who would
wish to erect a theory on such founda-
tions? And what do we gain from the classifications Tragedy, Comedy, History,
Pastoral, Tragical-Historical, Historical-
Pastoral, Pastoral-Comical, and Comical-
Historical–Pastoral? And even were we to
shuffle those "-cals" a hundred times,
what would we be left with in the end?
Not a single one of Shakespeare's plays
would be a Greek Tragedy, Comedy, Pastoral, nor should it be. Each play is History
in the broadest sense, which is of course
tinged to a greater or lesser degree with
tragedy, comedy, and so on, but the colors

are so infinitely varied that in the end each play remains and must remain *what it is: History! A heroic drama bringing to life the fortunes of the nation during the Middle Ages!* Or (with the exception of a few *divertissements* and plays in the proper sense) a complete *enactment of a world event, of a human destiny possessed of grandeur.*

Sadder and more important is the thought that even this great creator of history and the world soul grows older every day, that the words and customs and categories of the age wither and fall like autumnal leaves, that we are already so far removed from these great ruins of the age of chivalry that even Garrick, the reviver of Shakespeare and the guardian angel of his grave, is obliged to amend, cut, and mutilate so much of his work. And soon perhaps, as everything becomes effaced

and tends in different directions, even his
drama will become quite incapable of living performance, will become the dilapi-
dated remains of a colossus, of a pyramid,
which all gaze upon with wonder and
none understands. I count myself lucky
that I still live in the last days of an age
when I could understand him; and when
you, my friend, who feel and recognize
yourself when you read him, and whom I
have embraced more than once before his
sacred image, when you can still nurture
the sweet dream worthy of your gifts, a
dream that you will erect a monument to
him in our degenerate land, *drawn from our
own age of chivalry* and written in our language. I envy you that dream; may your
noble German powers not let up until the
wreath is hanging aloft. And should you

later see how the ground quakes beneath
your edifice, and around it the vulgar
masses stand and gape or scoff, and the ev-
erlasting pyramids cannot reawaken the
spirit of ancient Egypt—your work will
endure; and a faithful successor will seek
out your grave and write with devoted
hand the words that describe the lives of
almost all the men of merit in the world:

Voluit! quiescit!

Editor's Notes

First published in *Von deutscher Art und Kunst* (Hamburg, 1773). The text is based on *Shakespeare*, in *Schriften zur Ästhetik und Literatur, 1767–1781*, ed. Günter E. Grimm, vol. 2 of Johann Gottfried Herder, *Werke* (Frankfurt am Main: Deutscher Klassiker Verlag, 1993), 498–521.

If any man . . . image: an allusion to Mark Akenside, *The Pleasures of the Imagination* (1744), 3:550–59:

> Hence when lightning fires
> The arch of heav'n, and thunders rock the ground,

When furious whirlwinds rend the
   howling air,
And ocean, groaning from his lowest bed,
Heaves his tempest'ous billows to the sky;
Amid the mighty uproar, while below
The nations tremble, Shakespeare looks
   abroad
From some high cliff superior, and enjoys
The elemental war. . . .

What a library: for example, John Dryden's *An Essay of Dramatick Poesie* (1668), Pope's preface to his edition of *The Works of Shakespeare* (1726), Edward Young's *Conjectures on Original Composition* (1759), Henry Home's *Elements of Criticism* (1762–65), Samuel Johnson's preface to his edition of *The Plays of William Shakespeare* (1747), and Elizabeth Montagu's *Essay on the Writings and Genius of Shakespear* (1769); and in France: Voltaire's remarks in his *Lettres*

écrites de Londres sur les Anglois et autres sujets
(1734); in Germany: Johann Elias Schlegel's
Vergleichung Shakespears und Andreas Gryphs
(1741), Wilhelm Heinrich von Gerstenberg's *Briefe über Merkwürdigkeiten der Litteratur*, nos. 14–18 (1766), Lessing in *Letters
Concerning Recent Literature* (1759) and in
Hamburg Dramaturgy (1767); Johann Joachim Eschenburg, who translated Hurd and
Montagu (1771).

Shakespeare's boldest friends: for example, Pope,
Johnson, and Gerstenberg.

the rules: the three classical unities of time, place,
and action.

dithyramb: According to Aristotle tragedy origi-
nated in an introductory tale improvised by
the leader of the chorus, the purpose of
which was to state the theme that the dithyramb, a hymn sung to the god Diony-
sos, would elaborate (*Poetics* 4.1449a14–15).

Herder's account of the development of Greek tragedy follows that of Aristotle.

simplicity of Greek plot: Aristotle distinguishes between simple and complex plots and demands that the "successful plot" of a tragedy must have "a single and not . . . a double issue" (trans. W. Hamilton Pye [London: Heinemann, 1956] 13.1453a6).

buskined: Buskins were the high, thick-soled boots worn by actors in ancient Athenian tragedy; hence *buskined* means "dignified, elevated, lofty."

the artificiality of the rules . . . Nature!: The theory (as embodied in Aristotle) and practice of art (Sophocles) in Greece together constitute a unity, emerging naturally as the consequence of historical conditions. Aristotle did not "invent" his theory but merely discovered certain organic laws.

the art of the Greek poets . . . ascribe to them: Herder's target here is Lessing, who in section

46 of his *Hamburg Dramaturgy* had argued that the Greek tragedians simplified originally complex plots for the sake of the unities of time and place.

the previous dithyrambic feeling: that is, the idea of a simple, single scene.

Thespis: a Greek poet of the sixth century BC, traditionally credited with the invention of tragedy. He introduced an actor separated from the chorus and the dialogue between the leader of the chorus and this actor.

excellent chapter on the nature of plot: *Poetics* 7. Aristotle writes that "the proper limit" of plot length is "the magnitude which admits of a change from good fortune to bad, in a sequence of events which follow one another either inevitably or according to probability" (*Poetics* 7.1451a12).

the so-called dramatic rules . . . Aristotle: by Corneille (*Discours des trois unités*, 1660), Boileau (*Ars poétique*, 1674), and René Le Bossu

(*Traité du poème épique*, 1674), but also by German imitators such as Johann Christoph Gottsched in his *Critische Dichtkunst* (1740).

Lessing: *Hamburg Dramaturgy*, §§ 36–50 (1767).

Spanish-Senecan heroes: an allusion to the sources of the French tragedians Corneille (his *Cid* was based on the drama *The Youthful Deeds of Cid* by Guillen de Castro and Seneca's *Cinna*) and Racine (his *Phèdre* was inspired by Seneca's *Phaedra*). Corneille and Racine saw themselves as continuing the later Euripidean and Senecan tradition of tragedy, whereas Herder views Sophocles as the apotheosis of tragic drama.

galimatias: confused language, meaningless talk, nonsense.

Aristotle has declared it to be: Aristotle's theory of the cathartic effect of tragedy, which consists in arousing the purgative emotions of fear and pity (*Poetics* 6.1449b2–3).

"two-hour performance": as demanded by Corneille in his *Discours des trois unités*. Lessing, like Herder, also criticizes the Frenchman for following the letter of Aristotle's rules but not the spirit of drama (*Hamburg Dramaturgy*, § 45).

national institution: an allusion to the fact that Greek tragedies were performed as religious celebrations in Athens.

Crébillon: Prosper Jolyot de Crébillon (1674–1762), a rival of Voltaire who wrote tragedies based on classical and mythological sources such as *Idoménée* (1705) and *Rhadamiste et Zénobie* (1711).

Astrea: *L'Astrée* was a pastoral romance by Honoré d'Urfé (1567–1625) which appeared between 1607 and 1627.

Clélies *and* Aspasias: Clélie is the eponymous heroine of Mademoiselle de Scudéry's (1607–1701) *Clélie*, a ten-volume, pseudohistorical romance that was published between 1654 and 1660. Aspasia, originally a Greek courtesan and later the wife of Pericles, gave her name to several eighteenth-century French novels, as well as to a tale by Christoph Martin Wieland (1733–1813) sending up the French literature of love and society.

toto divisis ab orbe Britannis: the Britons, divided from the rest of the world; after Virgil *Ecologues* 1.66.

pullulus Aristotelis: pupil of Aristotle (literally "chicken").

since . . . genius is more than philosophy . . . analyzer. Cf. Young, *Thoughts:* "§ 138 By the praise of Genius we detract not from Learning [. . .] § 141 Learning we thank, Genius we revere; That gives us pleasure, This gives us rapture; That informs, This inspires; and is itself inspired; for Genius is from Heaven, Learning from man [. . .] § 142 Learning is borrowed knowledge; Genius is knowledge innate, and quite our own. § 143 Therefore, as *Bacon* observes, it may take a nobler name, and be called Wisdom; in which sense of wisdom, some are born wise."

Home. . . Johnson: Henry Home, Lord Kames (1696–1782), author of *Elements of Criticism*, (1762); Richard Hurd (1720–1808), whose translation of Horace's *Ars poetica* (1749) contained a commentary in which the different kinds of drama were analyzed; Alexander Pope's edition of Shakespeare of 1725 defended the poet against charges of having misapplied the Aristotelian rules; in the foreword to his own edition of Shakespeare in 1765, Samuel Johnson characterized Shakespeare as a natural genius who is permitted to ignore all rules.

plot, character, thought, language, song making, *and* spectacle: the six elements of tragedy, as outlined by Aristotle in *Poetics* 6.1450b19–28.

interpreter of Nature: an allusion to Bacon's notion of the *homo minister et interpres naturae*, the human being as the servant and interpreter of Nature.

Lear: *King Lear*, 1.1.

the strictest rule of your Aristotle: Aristotle demands that tragedy represent a single, whole action (*Poetics* 8).

Two aged fathers: Lear and Gloucester. The construction of the plot of *King Lear* defies Aristotle's ban on plots with a "double issue" (*Poetics* 13).

Blind Gloucester: *King Lear*, 4.6.

Father Aristotle: *Poetics* 7.

Lessing compared: in *Hamburg Dramaturgy*, §§ 11–12, where Lessing compares Voltaire's use of the ghost in his *Semiramis* with Shakespeare's in *Hamlet*.

Shakespeare is Sophocles' brother. Cf. Young: "§ 295 *Shakespeare* mingled no water with his wine, lower'd his Genius by no vapid Imitation. § 296 *Shakespeare* gave us a *Shakespeare*, nor could the first in antient fame have given us more. §297 *Shakespeare* is not their Son, but Brother; their Equal, and that, in spite of all his faults."

Spinoza's vast god: Together with Lessing and Goethe, Herder helped stimulate the enormous interest in Spinoza's pantheism in Germany. Spinoza's God, who is identical to nature, also moves in Shakespeare's plays.

sportive Frenchman: Voltaire, who criticized Shakespeare in *Essai sur la poésie épique* (1728) and *Lettres sur les Anglais* (1734).

Shakespeare . . . foolishness: an allusion to 1 Corinthians 1:23.

What do we mean by time *and* place *anyway?*: Herder's criticisms are here directed at

Corneille's arguments in *Discours sur les trois unités* 3, where he demands that the length of the performance exactly match that of the action represented on the stage.

Savoyard of the theater: a posturer, mountebank.

Mahomet's dream: Muhammad's vision of the beauties of Paradise.

ordine successivorum et simultaneorum: order of succession and simultaneity.

Cacklogallinian: a race of giant, intelligent fowl in Samuel Brunt's satire *A Voyage to Cacklogallinia with a Description of the Religion, Policy, Customs and Manners of that Country* (1727), a work that many in eighteenth-century Germany, including Herder, falsely attributed to Swift. Here Herder punningly associates this land of clucking scholars with France (the Latin name of which was "Gallia").

Warburton: William Warburton's (1698–1779) eight-volume edition of Shakespeare (1747).

author of the . . . essay: The "him" is actually a
    "her": Elizabeth Montagu (1720–1800),
    founder of the Bluestocking Club. Herder
    reviewed the German translation of her
    Essay on the Writings and Genius of Shakespear
    (1769) in 1771.

a writer . . . feeling for Shakespeare: Heinrich Wil-
    helm von Gerstenberg's (1737–1823) *Ver-
    such über Shakespeares Werke und Genie* (Essay
    on Shakespeare's Works and Genius) ap-
    peared in his *Briefe über Merkwürdigkeiten der
    Litteratur*, second collection (not third, as in
    Herder's footnote), nos. 14–18 (Letters on
    the Curiosities of Literature, 1766). Ger-
    stenberg's bizarre attempt to classify Shake-
    speare's dramas according to the categories
    of Polonius in *Hamlet*, 2.2 can be found in
    letter 17 and was the main target of Herder's
    criticism in the first draft of his essay in 1771.

honest fishmonger . . . gray beard . . . weak hams:
    Polonius in *Hamlet*, 2.2.176 and 201–4.

the series of "-als" and "-cals": Polonius speaks of
"tragedy, comedy, history, pastoral, pastoral-comical, historical-pastoral-tragical-his-
torical, tragical-comical-historical-pastoral"
(2.2.398–401).

locos communes: commonplaces.

Stobaeus: Johannes Stobaeus (fifth century AD)
compiled various series of extracts of Greek
authors, one of which is known as *Florilegium* and served as a model for later cornu-
copias. The "new" Stobaeus is William
Dodd's anthology *The Beauties of Shakespeare*
(1752), which was widely read in Germany
also (by Goethe, among others). J. J. Eschenburg (1743–1820), one of Shakespeare's
German translators, planned a similar anthology in German.

Lancelot . . . king of knights: fools in Shake-
speare's plays. "Lancelot" is Lancelot
Gobbo, Shylock's servant in *Merchant of
Venice*, "clowns and jesters" refers to figures

such as Feste in *Twelfth Night* and Touchstone in *As You Like It*; "poor Richard" is the inept monarch in *Richard II*; the "king of knights" is the buffoonish Sir John Falstaff in *Henry IV, Parts I and II*.

the great baby . . . "time is time": "great baby" (*Hamlet*, 2.2.384), "clouds for camels" (3.2.365), "played Julius Caesar" (3.2.95–100), "why day is day" (2.2.89).

a few divertissements *and plays in the proper sense*: Herder himself uses the English word "play" here, in the sense of "interlude."

Garrick: David Garrick (1717–79) created a more naturalistic method of acting and went back to the original, uncut Shakespeare texts. In 1769, in Stratford, he organized a Shakespeare festival, which awakened new interest in Shakespeare.

you, my friend: that is, Goethe. His "monument" is *Götz von Berlichingen*, a drama set in Germany's own "age of chivalry," which

Goethe sent to Herder at the end of 1771. Herder looks to Goethe to take up the challenge of Shakespeare at this turning point in the development of German dramatic literature.

Voluit! quiescit!: "He has striven! Now he rests!"

Index

action, 8–10, 11–12, 13, 30, 31, 50, 55
Addison, Joseph, xxii
Aeschylus, 6, 8, 11
Aristotle, xv, xxv, 7, 12, 13, 14, 21, 30, 35, 37

Borck, Kaspar Wilhelm, xii–xiii

chorus, xxv, 6–7, 10, 11, 25
Corneille, Pierre, xv, xxvi, 2, 16, 18, 23
Crébillon, Prosper Jolyot de, 23

dithyramb, xxv, 11, 25
d'Urfé, Honoré, 23

Enlightenment, xx, xxxi, xxxiv

Euripides, 2, 7, 12

fear and pity, xv, 21, 28

Flachsland, Caroline, xvii

Garrick, David, 63

genius, xix, xxi–xxii, xxx, xxxvii, 28

Germany, ix–xi

Gerstenberg, Heinrich Wilhelm von, xvi, xviii, xx, xxiii, xxxvii, 60–62

Goethe, Johann Gottfried, xli

Gottsched, Johann Christoph, xii–xiii

Greek tragedy, xiii, xv, xxv–xxvi, 6–15, 25, 28

Hamann, Johann Georg, xvii, xx

Hamlet, 45–46

history, xxxi–xxxiv, xl–xli, 29–30, 32, 62–63

Home, Henry (Lord Kames), 30, 60

Homer, xix, xxxix, 30

Hurd, Richard, 30

illusion, xxix, 21, 40–41, 49, 52, 56–58

Johnson, Samuel, xxvii n, 30
Julius Caesar, xii

King Lear, 33–37, 58

Lessing, Gotthold Ephraim, xiv–xv, xviii, xxiii,
    17, 45

Macbeth, 41–45
Macpherson, James, ix, xl
Mahomet (Muhammad), 56
Möser, Justus, ix

nature, 10, 14, 26–27, 32, 49–50, 57
neoclassicism, xii, xxvi, 16–24, 48, 52–53
Nicolai, Friedrich, xiv

Ossian, viii, xix, xl
Othello, 38–39, 47

place, 10, 40–41, 45, 50
plot. *See* action
Polonius, xxxviii, 60–62

Pope, Alexander, xxxix, 30

Racine, Jean, xiv, xxvi, 16, 18

Schiller, Friedrich, xxxv
Schlegel, Johann Elias, xiii–xiv
Sophocles, xxv, xxx, 2, 5–6, 7, 8–9, 11, 12, 13, 24,
    30, 31, 32, 46, 49, 50
Spinoza, Baruch, xxxiv
Stobaeus, Johannes, 61

Thespis, 13
time, 10, 40–41, 45, 50, 51–58

Volkspoesie, xx
Voltaire, xii, xxvi, 2, 16, 18, 23

Warburton, William, 59
Wieland, Christoph Martin, xviii
Winckelmann, Johann Joachim, xxvii

Young, Edward, xxi, xxx

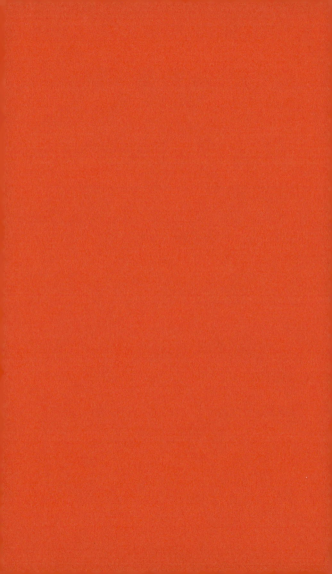